of *The Hardening Ground*

"In this, his first collection, Shaun Traynor with twenty two poems and an extended Meditation on the Suspension of Stormont takes his place among his peers from the North of Ireland and the South."

— Desmond O'Grady, *Hibernia Review of Books*

of *Images in Winter*

"Shaun Traynor's book is a delight. The writing here is fresh and exact; the mood is one of accurate celebration tempered with caution. The poetry is an act of faith, the rhythm a gift of grace."

— Robert Welch, *Literary Review*

of his writing for children

"*The Giants' Olympics*... is instantly successful, a very funny book by an accomplished storyteller."

— Mike Maran, *The Guardian*

of *A Little Man in England*

"This is a memorable book which all six reviewers (7-11 yrs) loved."

— Lesley Reece, *Books Ireland*

"Shaun Traynor's writing (for children) exudes love and tenderness towards children and their earth. His modern fairytales with their contempory settings capture children's imagination from the beginning."

— *Irish Children's Book Trust Guide to Children's Books Decade 1980-90*

The Poolbeg Book of
Irish Poetry for Children

The Poolbeg Book of Irish Poetry for Children

Collected by Shaun Traynor

POOLBEG

FOR CHILDREN

Published 1997
by Poolbeg Press Ltd
123 Baldoyle Industrial Estate
Dublin 13, Ireland

© Shaun Traynor 1997

The moral right of the authors has been asserted.

The Publishers gratefully acknowledge the support of The Arts Council.

A catalogue record for this book is available from the British Library.

ISBN 1 85371 726 6

Illustrations by Marianne Lee
Cover design by Poolbeg Group Services Ltd
Set by Poolbeg Group Services Ltd in AGaramond 11/13
Printed by The Guernsey Press Ltd,
Vale, Guernsey, Channel Islands.

About our editor

Shaun Traynor is a Northern Irish poet and children's novelist. He is London based, but hopes to return to Ireland one day.

My thanks to:

Gavin Henderson in whose beautifully appointed flat in Brighton, England, this book surely took shape.

Ursula Traynor for her researches in Dungannon Library in Co. Tyrone and for her advice as the project moved forward.

Louise Grainger and other staff at the Poetry Library in The South Bank Centre, London SE1.

Alan Slingsby for access to his computer suite in North London.

Nicole Jussek, my editor at Children's Poolbeg, who kept a steady hand on the tiller.

Shaun Traynor
London 1997

for Evelyn O'Reilly and Rowan O'Reilly,
spanning the generations

Contents

SECTION III: FROM THE POETS OF TODAY

 *Introduction*

I was walking with a friend recently and I said to him that I was thinking of putting together a collection of Irish poetry for children. He said, "There isn't any."

I think what he meant was that there is much Irish poetry which is suitable for children but very little written actually for children.

Now I knew what my task should be – to find out just how many poems there are in the Irish literary canon which could be thought of as suitable for children or – even better – actually written for children and bring them together in one book; a book of exclusively Irish poetry for children.

My quest was to find out if we did have an Eleanor Farjeon, a Robert Frost, a Hilaire Belloc, a Lewis Carrol, a Robert Louis Stevenson, a Walter de la Mare, a James Kirkup, a Roger McGough and so on. I mention Eleanor Farjeon first because my favourite children's poet and my favourite lines of hers have in fact become the lines of a hymn:

Morning has broken
Like the first morning,
Blackbird has spoken
Like the first bird –

There is a freshness about those first two lines, a sense of something happening for the first time, which defines poetry. It was therefore with a feeling of celebration that I greeted the work of Cecil Frances Alexander, wife of the Archbishop of Armagh, Sunday school teacher in Strabane, and author of "All Things Bright and Beautiful", "Once in Royal David's City" and "There is a Green Hill Far Away". It was a very good start.

With the noble poems of Francis Ledwidge and the charming, direct and utterly amusing poems of James Stephens, I felt that with these three poets as a basis for an anthology I was getting into something very worthwhile indeed.

Then of course there were Yeats and Kavanagh and Seamus

Heaney to consider; to see them as "back-up" was an amusing concept and it made me realise that by putting different criteria on poets' work I could and would come up with some interesting results, maybe almost surreal. I couldn't resist thinking at that point of a painting I had once seen showing a surrealist map of the world with all the countries in their correct place but all of them the wrong size, for instance Ireland might be really big on the map, Britain really small, America small, the West Indies huge and so on. I quickly came to realise that this "surrealist map" principle would work beyond an actual map of poets, it would affect the choice of poems within each poet's canon. Leafing through a collection of a famous poet's poems I would be looking for a poem which would amuse or delight a child, not one which would speak directly to an adult in an adult way. Maybe we could find some which would be one and the same.

I know the work of Patrick Kavangh well and have read his collected works many times but I didn't retain a memory of his "Four Birds". Maybe this was because when reading his poems I was looking for something understandably adult or something which suited my adult needs at the time and a poem about four birds wasn't it. I had passed it over, that is until now. I knew most of Yeats of course but I hadn't registered much with "To a Squirrel at Kyle-Na-No" which is the obvious Yeats' poem with which to lead in an anthology of poetry for children. It was also interesting to be able to indicate that both John Hewitt and Louis MacNeice had written a poem called "The Pet Shop" but I knew there was also a responsibility to print, alongside these "newly sighted" poems, a representation of the work for which the poet was best known. So the surrealist map had to be taken down from the wall and some kind of common sense or balance be brought into the enterprise. It would be wrong for a child to be introduced to the work of Patrick Kavanagh only by "Four Birds" and not glimpse "A Christmas Childhood"; wrong to print "To a Squirrel at Kyle-Na-No" without at least some of Yeats' better known poems alongside.

With Kavanagh and Yeats this didn't present a problem but with some of the other poets in Section II I did have problems finding poems which could genuinely speak to a child. I was looking for some kind of lyrical grace or ambiguity which can render a poem instantly universal or I was looking for simplicity and innocence of subject matter. Yet I was aware that more complex poems have an essential place in a child's literary development. I was becoming at this stage too preoccupied by anxieties about what a child could or could not assimilate and accommodate. It was time to bring in children themselves as arbiters.

I tested all these poems with nine- and ten-year-olds in different schools. What I did was to give the class a copy of several poems and asked them to read the poems, copy them out and then illustrate them. No teacher assistance was given. The poems had to speak to the children on their own merits or not. Some of the drawings were very astute. There was a terrific one of Patrick Kavanagh standing on a hill top shouting, "I LOVE MONAGHAN!" There was another of a priest (or clergyman) in Belfast hurrying away down a street and children shouting after him, "DON'T BE A BIGOT!" Often the children's views were at odds with my own judgement and this made me consider my selections all the more carefully. One poem in this anthology was voted number one by all children on every test and this was "How High?"

"Do I have to make it rhyme, sir?"

"Why is poetry different nowadays?"

These are the two questions I am asked most consistently by children and teachers when I visit schools. I will answer these questions now, briefly, because we have in my anthology examples of many different kinds of poetry, all co-exist.

The answer to question one is quite simply, "No. You don't have to make it rhyme." Poets today use a lot of different forms. They have that freedom. However, it's fair to say, in children's poetry, more often than not, poets tend to use rhyme where they wouldn't dream of using it in their adult work. This is

3

worrying since it gives children quite the wrong impression of where poetry is at. It is a tentative ambition of this anthology to break down prejudice and show models of very many different types of poem and innovations of form. This frees the child to express herself or himself in a variety of different ways. Or find a new way. No, it doesn't have to rhyme.

The answer to question two, "Why is poetry different nowadays?" is a bit more complex. During the first world war, in other words almost a century ago, poetry changed. Soldier-poets confronted with the horrors of war wanted to change the language of poetry into something more direct. They wanted to get away from the comfort of archaic language, recognisable form and rhyme. At the same time in London a group of intellectuals called The Imagists were working along parallel lines and they actually set down a list of rules as to how they thought poetry should change. Their ideas derived from a French innovation called *vers libre,* free verse. The rules they came up with included: to write *vers libre,* in other words compose in the sequence of the musical phrase and not in the sequence of the metronome; to use the language of common speech, to allow complete freedom of choice in subject matter. This manifesto was written in 1917 but no poet writing since has been unaware of it. Poets in Ireland and Britain were quick to pick up on this innovation as musicians and painters were also quick to pick up on innovations in their own fields. Society itself changed dramatically. All of art changed radically before 1930, yet in some schools in Britain and Ireland today, some teachers still teach the old poetry in the old way.

If the last bit of this introduction has been hectoring or pedagogical I apologise. It was aimed at teachers. Really what I want to happen with this book is for children and adults to read these poems aloud over and over again, let the voice educate the mind.

Shaun Traynor 1997

Section I

From Ancient Ireland

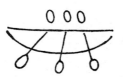

The Hermit's Song

A hiding tuft, a green-barked yew-tree
is my roof,
While nearby a great oak keeps me
Tempest-proof.

I can pick my fruit from an apple-tree
Like an inn,
Or can fill my fist where hazels
Shut me in.

A clear well beside me offers
Best of drink,
And there grows a bed of cresses
Near its brink.

Pigs and goats, the friendliest neighbours,
Nestle near,
Wild swine come, or broods of badgers,
Grazing deer.

All the gentry of the county
Come to call
And the foxes come behind them,
Best of all.

To what meals the woods invite me
All about!
There are water, herbs and cresses,
Salmon, trout.

A clutch of eggs, sweet mast and honey
Are my meat.
Heath berries and whortleberries
For a sweet.

All that one could ask for comfort
Round me grows,
There are hips and hews and strawberries,
Nuts and sloes.

And when summer spreads its mantle
What a sight!
Marjoram and leeks and pignuts,
Juicy, bright.

Dainty redbreasts briskly forage
Every bush,
Round and round my hut there flutter
Swallow, thrush.

Bees and beetles, music makers,
Croon and strum;
Geese pass over, duck in autumn,
Dark streams hum.

Angry wren, officious linnet
And black-cap,
All industrious, and the woodpecker's
Sturdy tap.

From the sea the gulls and herons
Flutter in,
While in upland heather rises
The grey hen.

In the year's most brilliant weather
Heifers low
Through green fields, not driven nor beaten,
Tranquil, slow.

In wreathed boughs the wind is whispering,
Skies are blue,
Swans call, river water falling
Is calling too.

Anonymous
Trans Frank O'Connor

Four Seasons

Winter

Deep winter is the darkest of seasons;
Stormy waves beat upon the earth's shores.
Sad all the birds of the plan
except the bloody deep red raven
at the harsh sounds of winter.
Black, dark, smoky season.
Bone-gnawing hounds are arrogant;
The iron pot is placed above the fire
on a dark black day.

Spring

Raw, cold, icy spring;
coldness is conceived in its wind,
ducks freeze to ponds,
the harsh cry of the wildly complaining crane
is heard by stags in woodland wastes
at the morning's early dawning.
Birds are awoken from islands,
many are the wild animals from which they fly
out of the wood, out of the green grass.

Summer

Summer is suitable for long journeys;
calm are the tall, choice trees
unstirred by the wind.

The plumage of the sheltering wood is green,
treacherous waters are diminished.
A favourable omen in the good earth.

Autumn

Autumn is a suitable season for staying put,
there is a load for each person's horse
in the abundance of the so-short days.
Speckled fauns follow behind elegant hinds
among the sheltering red stalks of the bracken.
Stags hurry from high ground
hearing the clamour of the herd.

Acorns and berries in the peaceful woods;
cornstalks in coinfields
across the face of the brown earth.
Blackthorn and thorny briars
by the rampart of the ruined habitation;
the failing earth is full with heavy tree-fruit,
nuts fall: the fine fruits of the hazel wood,
of the great trees of the ramparts.

Anonymous
Trans Seán Hutton

Colum Cille's Farewell To Ireland

If all Scotland were mine,
from boundary to boundary,
I'd prefer to build my house
in the middle of sweet Derry.

The reasons I love Derry,
its plain, its brightness,
and the number of fair angels
from one end to the other.

There's not a tree on the plain
of comely wooded Derry
without fledgling angels
two to each leaf.

Sorrow to me the weeping
from all sides of Lough Foyle;
the cries of the people of Eoin, of Conall,
lamenting my departure.

Having left my own kinsmen,
I won't make any secret:
there will be no night – there's no denying –
when I shall not be weeping.

As to my parting from the Gael,
to whom my love was given,
if I live but one night away from them
that matters to me little.

I myself am of the Gael
of the Gael my honour;
of the Gael my learning
of the men of Ireland my beauty.

Having heard your lamenting
why am I still living?
great cry of the people of Derry
which broke my heart in quarters.

Acorn abounding Derry behind us
sorrowful, tearful, dispirited;
departing torments the heart,
and going amidst a foreign people.

Great the speed of my currach
its stern towards Derry;
distressing my journey on the high sea
towards coast-girt Scotland.

I look back over the waves
to the plain of luxuriant oaks;
great the tears of the soft grey eye
turned back towards Ireland.

There is a grey eye
that will look back towards Ireland;
that will not ever again see
Ireland's men or women.

Morning and noon I lament,
alas the journey I make!
my name, I don't conceal it:
'Back turned towards Ireland'.

Bear my greetings westward;
my heart is broken in my breast;
when my meeting with death takes place
it will be for love for the Gael!

Colum Cille
Trans Seán Hutton

I've News For You

I've news for you:
the stag bellows,
winter's snow,
summer's gone;

high cold wind,
sun low in sky,
short days,
heavy seas;

deep red bracken's
skeletal form,
barnacle goose's
customed call;

cold has seized
the bird's wings,
icy season:
that's my news.

Anonymous
Trans Seán Hutton

The Scholar and His Cat

I and Pangur, my white cat,
each has his appointed task:
his mind is set on hunting
and mine on my special skill.

More than fame it's quiet I love,
studious at my wondrous book;
while Pangur's never envious,
loving his own childish craft.

Home together, just we two
– boredom never enters in –
we find enjoyment without end
in sharpening our skills.

Sometimes, after hard onset,
a mouse is captured in his net;
and as for me, in mine there falls
a dictum of difficult interpretation.

He fixes a bright, faultless eye
on the enclosing wall;
I focus my keen but feeble eye
on prickly points of learning.

A mouse clasped in his sharp-clawed paw,
rejoicing, he moves swiftly;
I rejoice in the resolution
of a rare and abstruse problem.

While this is our wonted routine
neither hinders the other;
each finds his calling good,
each one enjoys himself.

Each is master of the task
which he performs daily;
for my work I am well suited,
bringing light to dark places.

Anonymous
Trans Seán Hutton

Icham of Irlaunde

Icham of Irlaunde
Ant of the holy londe of irlonde
Gode sir pray ich ye
for of salute charite,
come ant daunce wyt me,
in irlaunde.

Anonymous

Section II

The Poets of the Past

from *Ode*

We are the music-makers
And we are the dreamers of dreams,
Wandering by lone sea-breakers,
And sitting by desolate streams;
World-losers and worldforsakers,
On whom the pale moon gleams:
Yet we are the movers and shakers
Of the world for ever, it seems.

Arthur O'Shaughnessy

from *The Village Schoolmaster*

Beside yon straggling fence that skirts the way,
With blossom'd furze unprofitably gay,
There, in his noisy mansion, skilled to rule,
The village master taught his little school.
A man severe he was, and stern to view;
I knew him well, and every truant knew:
Well had the boding tremblers learned to trace
The day's disasters in his morning face;
Full well they laughed with counterfeited glee
At all his jokes, for many a joke had he;
Full well the busy whisper circling round
Conveyed the dismal tidings when he frowned.
Yet he was kind, or, if severe in aught,
The love he bore to learning was in fault;
The village all declared how much he knew:
'Twas certain he could write, and cypher too;
Lands he could measure, terms and tides presage,
And e'en the story ran that he could guage:
In arguing, too, the parson owned his skill;
For e'en though vanquished, he could argue still;
While words of learned length and thundering sound
Amazed the gazing rustics ranged around;
And still they gazed, and still the wonder grew,
That one small head could carry all he knew.
But past is all his fame. The very spot
Where many a time he triumphed, is forgot.

Oliver Goldsmith

A Riddle

We are little airy Creatures,
All of different Voice and Features,
One of us in Glass is set,
One of us you'll find in Jet,
T'other you may see in Tin,
And the fourth a Box within,
If the fifth you shou'd pursue
It can never fly from you.

Jonathan Swift

[A. The Vowels]

All Things Bright and Beautiful

All things bright and beautiful
All creatures great and small,
All things wise and wonderful,
The Lord God made them all.

Each little flower that opens,
Each little bird that sings,
He made their glowing colours,
He made their tiny wings.
The purple-headed mountain,
The river running by,
The sunset, and the morning,
That brightens up the sky;

The cold wind in the winter,
The pleasant summer sun,
The ripe fruits in the garden,
He made them every one.
He gave us eyes to see them,
And lips that we might tell,
How great is God Almighty,
Who has made all things well.

Cecil Frances Alexander

The Fieldmouse

Where the acorn tumbles down,
Where the ash tree sheds its berry,
With your fur so soft and brown,
With your eye so round and merry,
Scarcely moving the long grass,
Fieldmouse, I can see you pass.

Little thing, in what dark den,
Lie you all the winter sleeping
Till warm weather comes again?
Then once more I see you peeping
Round about the tall tree roots,
Nibbling at their fallen fruits.

Fieldmouse, fieldmouse, do not go,
Where the farmer stacks his treasure,
Find the nut that falls below,
Eat the acorn at your pleasure,
But you must not steal the grain
He has stacked with so much pain.
Make your hole where mosses spring,
Underneath the tall oak's shadow.

Pretty, quiet, harmless thing,
Play about the sunny meadow.
Keep away from corn and house,
None will harm you, little mouse.

Cecil Frances Alexander

Beasts and Birds

The dog will come when he is called,
The cat will walk away;
The monkey's cheek is very bald,
The goat is fond of play.
The parrot is a prate-apace,
Yet knows not what she says;
The noble horse will win the race,
Or draw you in a chaise.
The pig is not a feeder nice,
The squirrel loves a nut,
The wolf would eat you in a trice,
The buzzard's eyes are shut.
The lark sings high up in the air,
The linnet in the tree;
The swan he has a bosom fair,
And who so proud as he?

Adelaide O'Keeffe

The Kite

My kite is three feet broad, and six feet long;
The standard straight, the bender tough and strong,
And to its milk-white breast five painted stars belong.
Grand and majestic soars my paper kite,
Through trackless skies it takes its lofty flight:
Nor lark nor eagle flies to such a noble height.
As in the field I stand and hold the twine,
Swift I unwind, to give it length of line,
Yet swifter it ascends, nor will to earth incline.
Like a small speck, so high I see it sail,
I hear its pinions flutter in the gale,
And, like a flock of wild geese,
sweeps its flowing tail.

Adelaide O'Keeffe

The Comical Child

Have you heard about Marigold,
The girl who was young before she was old?
Just over her mouth was an elegant nose,
And inside her slippers she carried ten toes.
And (this is what really made people stare)
The top of her head was covered with hair.
People who knew her from childhood have said
That she fell fast asleep every night in her bed.
Moreover – and this must occasion tremendous
surprise –
When sleeping she always shut tight both her eyes.
She could be cross, and she could be mild –
Mercy me! What a comical child!
And let me say this with the fullest authority
Her real name was Marigold, not Mary Dorothy.
For I'm speaking of Marigold, this is quite plain,
And not of Lucinda, or Noreen, or Jane.

Anonymous

Breakfast Time

The sun is always in the sky
Whenever I get out of bed,
And I often wonder why
It's never late. My sister said

She didn't know who did the trick,
And that she didn't care a bit,
And I should eat my porridge quick.
– I think its mother wakens it.

James Stephens

Midnight

And suddenly I wakened in a fright;
I thought I heard a movement in the room
But did not dare to look; I snuggled right
Down underneath the bedclothes – then a boom
And a tremendous voice said, "Sit up, lad,
And let me see your face." So up I sat,
Although I didn't want to –

I was glad I did though,
For it was an angel that had called me,
And he said, he'd come to know
Was I the boy who wouldn't say his prayers
Nor do his sums – and that I'd have to go
Straight down to hell because of such affairs:

I said I'd be converted and do good
If he would let me off – he said he would.

James Stephens

White Fields

I

In the winter time we go
Walking in the fields of snow;

Where there is no grass at all;
Where the top of every wall,

Every fence, and every tree,
Is as white as white can be.

II

Pointing out the way we came,
Every one of them the same –
All across the fields there be
Prints in silver filigree;

And our mothers always know,
By the footprints in the snow,

Where it is the children go.

James Stephens

The Snare

I hear a sudden cry of pain!
There is a rabbit in a snare:
Now I hear the cry again,
But I cannot tell from where.

But I cannot tell from where
He is calling out for aid!
Crying on the frightened air,
Making everything afraid!

Making everything afraid!
Wrinkling up his little face!
As he cries again for aid;
And I cannot find the place!

And I cannot find the place
Where his paw is in the snare!
Little One! Oh, Little One!
I am searching everywhere!

James Stephens

I Will Go With My Father A-Ploughing

I will go with my father a-ploughing
To the green field by the sea
And the rooks and the crows and the sea-gulls
Will come flocking after me.
I will sing to the patient horses,
With the lark in the white of the air,
And my father will sing the plough-share
That blesses the cleaving share.
I will go with my father a-ploughing
To the red field by the sea,
And the rooks and the gulls and the starlings
Will come flocking after me.
I will sing to the striding sowers,
With the finch on the greening sloe,
And my father will sing the seed-song
That only the wise men know.
I will go with my father a-reaping
To the brown field by the sea,
And the geese and the crows and the children
Will come flocking after me.
I will sing to the tan-faced reapers,
With the wren in the heat of the sun,
And my father will sing the scythe-song
That joys for the harvest done.

Joseph Campbell

The Ninepenny Fidil

My father and mother were Irish,
And I am Irish too;
I bought a wee fidil for ninepence,
And it is Irish, too.

I'm up in the morning early
To meet the dawn of day,
And to the lintwhites' piping
The many's the tune I play.

One pleasant eve in June-time
I met a lochrie-man:
His face and hands were weazen,
His height was not a span.

He boor'd me for my fidil –
"You know," says he, "like you,
My father and mother were Irish
And I am Irish, too!"

He gave me back my fidil,
My fidil-stick, also
And, stepping like a May-boy,
He jumped the Leargaidh Knowe.

I never saw him after,
Nor met his gentle kind;
But, whiles, I think I hear him
A-wheening in the wind!

My father and mother were Irish,
And I am Irish too;
I bought a wee fidil for ninepence,
And it is Irish, too.

I'm up in the morning early
To meet the dawn of day,
And to the lintwhites' piping
The many's the tune I play.

Joseph Campbell

The Summer-House

My summer-house
Is white with lime,
And roses climb
About the door,
And columbines
And gentle lady-flowers,
And fuchsias
And the carmine fairy-cap.
And rose-mallow
And red crow-toes,
And the fringed jessamine.
All day long
On the thorn before the door
The mellow blackbird pipes;
And thither echoes come
Of the long low wash of the sea,
And of the shy call
Of the hill-plover on the hill,
And of the plaintful song
Of the turf-cutters in the bog.

Oh, my house
Is a house of happiness,
My house
Is a house of love.

Joseph Campbell

Snapdragon

I love to see
The honey bee
Alight upon
The snapdragon,
And, hanging, grip
Its under lip
Pull its mouth wide,
Then slip inside
To steal anew
Of honey.dew.
But stealthily those
Lips then close,
Imprisoning
The adventurous thing;
And, even though
He will, I know,
In his own time
With art sublime,
Content and stout,
Squeeze himself out,
I hold my breath
Dreading his death,
That, ere he quit
His thieving, it
One day might hap
Some flaming snap-
Dragon might wake

To thought, and take
Umbrage at the
Marauding bee,
And while he sips
Might snap its lips
With gesture grim,
And swallow him.

Elizabeth Shane

An Old Waterford Woman

On the road over head,
To the passers-by
"Listen," she said,
"Inside this cliff are the dead.
They cry
Because they are dead."

"You hear," said I,
"The cry
Of the wind in the hollow face of the cliff:
Within the cliff
There is only earth."

"And what," she said
"Are the dead but earth?"

Mary Davenport O'Neill

Wishes

I'll take
The shallow loops the blackbirds make
In their low flight,
And gather the strange white
That changes a green field as night comes on;
I'll catch the bars of light,
Before they're gone,
That blinking eyes bring down from the moon,
And make my wishes out of these,
That if I please
I can dissolve them soon –
In time to save them from reality;
The toughness of its stuff would trouble me.

Mary Davenport O'Neill

Praise

Once with praising I was as tense
As a salmon must be at the salmon leap.
I was wound up to sweep
The world and sky and all experience,
And gather up some new extravagance.
Then, like a flash, I knew that all I'd tried
Was worse than nothing; that being stupified,
Oppressed, impressed, pressed under,
Blurred like the worm,
Dumb beneath a load of wonder,
At last was praise;
And staring on the ground
I sat limp-handed – swung full circle round.

Mary Davenport O'Neill

A Soft Day

A soft day, thank God!
A wind from the south
With a honeyed mouth;
A scent of drenching leaves,
Briar and beech and lime,
White elder-flower and thyme
And the soaking grass smells sweet,
Crushed by my two bare feet,
While the rain drips,
Drips, drips, drips from the eaves.

A soft day, thank God!
The hills wear a shroud
Of silver cloud;
The web the spider weaves
Is a glittering net;
The woodland path is wet,
And the soaking earth smells sweet
Under my two bare feet,
And the rain drips,
Drips, drips, drips from the leaves.

Winifred M Letts

The Bubble

See, the pretty Planet!
Floating sphere!
Faintest breeze will fan it
Far or near;

World as light as feather;
Moonshine rays,
Rainbow tints together,
As it plays;

Drooping, sinking, failing,
Nigh to earth,
Mounting, whirling, sailing,
Full of mirth;

Life there, welling, flowing,
Waving round;
Pictures coming, going,
Without sound.

Quick now, be this airy
Globe repelled!
Never can the fairy
Star be held.

Touched – it in a twinkle
Disappears!
Leaving but a sprinkle,
As of tears.

William Allingham

Swing, Swing

Swing, swing,
Sing, sing,
Here! my throne and I am a king!
Swing, sing,
Swing, sing,
Farewell, earth, for I'm on the wing!

Low, high,
Here I fly,
Like a bird through sunny sky;
Free, free,
Over the lea,
Over the mountain, over the sea!

Soon, soon,
Afternoon,
Over the sunset, over the moon;
Far, far,
Over all bar,
Sweeping on from star to star!

No, no,
Low, low,
Sweeping daisies with my toe,
Slow, slow,
To and fro,
Slow – slow – slow – slow.

William Allingham

Four Ducks on a Pond

Four ducks on a pond,
A grass-bank beyond,
A blue sky of spring,
White clouds on the wing:
What a little thing
To remember for years –
To remember with tears!

William Allingham

Japanese Print

Both skyed
In south-west wind beyond
Poplar and fir-tree, swallow,
Heron, almost collide,
Swerve
With a rapid
Dip of wing. Flap,
Each in an opposite curve.
Fork-tail, long neck outstretched
And feet. All happened
Above my head. The pair
Was disappearing. Say I
Had seen, half hint, a sketch on
Rice-coloured air.
Sharako, Hokusai!

Austin Clark

The Rann of the Little Playmate

Young Iosa plays with me every day.
(With an óró and an iaró)
Tig and Pookeen and Hide-in-the-Hay.
(With an óró and an iaró)
We race in the rivers with otters grey.
We climb the tall trees where the red squirrels play.
We watch the wee lady-bird fly far away.
(With an óró and an iaró and an umbo éró!)

Padraic Pearse

The Wayfarer

The beauty of the world hath made me sad,
This beauty that will pass;
Sometimes my heart hath shaken with great joy
To see a leaping squirrel in a tree,
Or a red lady-bird upon a stalk,
Or little rabbits in a field at evening,
Lit by a slanting sun,
Or some green hill where shadows drifted by,
Some quiet hill where mountainy man hath sown
And soon will reap, near to the gate of Heaven;
Or children with bare feet upon the sands
Of some ebbed sea, or playing on the streets
Of little towns in Connacht,
Things young and happy.
And then my heart hath told me:
These will pass,
Will pass and change, will die and be no more,
Things bright and green, things young and happy;
And I have gone upon my way
Sorrowful.

Padraic Pearse

To a Squirrel at Kyle-Na-No

Come play with me;
Why should you run
Through the shaking tree
As though I'd a gun
To strike you dead?
When all I would do
Is to scratch your head
And let you go.

WB Yeats

The Cat and the Moon

The cat went here and there
And the moon spun round like a top,
And the nearest kin of the moon,
The creeping cat, looked up.
Black Minnaloushe stared at the moon,
For, wander and wail as he would,
The pure cold light in the sky
Troubled his animal blood.
Minnaloushe runs in the grass
Lifting his delicate feet.
Do you dance, Minnaloushe, do you dance?
When two close kindred meet,
What better than call a dance?
Maybe the moon may learn,
Tired of that courtly fashion,
A new dance turn.
Minnaloushe creeps through the grass
From moonlit place to place,
The sacred moon overhead
Has taken a new phase.
Does Minnaloushe know that his pupils
Will pass from change to change,
And that from round to crescent,
From crescent to round they range?
Minnaloushe creeps through the grass
Alone, important and wise,
And lifts to the changing moon
His changing eyes.

WB Yeats

The Song of Wandering Aengus

I went out to the hazel wood,
Because a fire was in my head,
And cut and peeled a hazel wand,
And hooked a berry to a thread;
And when white moths were on the wing,
And moth-like stars were flickering out,
I dropped the berry in a stream
And caught a little silver trout.

When I had laid it on the floor
I went to blow the fire aflame,
But something rustled on the floor,
And some one called me by my name:
It had become a glimmering girl

With apple blossom in her hair
Who called me by my name and ran
And faded through the brightening air.

Though I am old with wandering
Through hollow lands and hilly lands,
I will find out where she has gone,
And kiss her lips and take her hands;
And walk among long dappled grass,
And pluck till time and times are done
The silver apples of the moon,
The golden apples of the sun.

WB Yeats

from *The Stolen Child*

Where dips the rocky highland
Of Sleuth Wood in the lake,
There lies a leafy island
Where flapping herons wake
The drowsy water-rats;
There we've hid our faery vats,
Full of berries
And of reddest stolen cherries.
Come away, O human child!
To the waters and the wild
With a faery, hand in hand,
For the world's more full of weeping
than you can understand.

Where the wave of moonlight glosses
The dim grey sands with light,
Far off by furthest Rosses
We foot it all the night,
Weaving olden dances,
Mingling hands and mingling glances
Till the moon has taken flight;
To and fro we leap
And chase the frothy bubbles,
While the world is full of troubles
And is anxious in its sleep.
Come away, O human child!
To the waters and the wild
With a faery, hand in hand,
For the world's more full of weeping
than you can understand.

WB Yeats

Lean Out of the Window

Lean out of the window,
Goldenhair,
I heard you singing
A merry air.

My book is closed,
I read no more,
Watching the fire dance
On the floor.

I have left my book:
I have left my room:
For I heard you singing
Through the gloom,

Singing and singing
A merry air.
Lean out of the window,
Goldenhair.

James Joyce

He Meditates on the Life of a Rich Man

A golden cradle under you, and you young;
A right mother and a strong kiss.

A lively horse, and you a boy;
A school and learning and close companions.

A beautiful wife, and you a man;
a wide house and everything that is good.

A fine wife, children, substance;
cattle, means, herds and flocks.

A place to sit, a place to lie down;
plenty of food and plenty of drink.

After that, an old man among old men;
Respect on you and honour on you.

Head of the court, of the jury, of the meeting,
And the counsellors not the worse for having you.

At the end of your days death, and then
Hiding away; the boards and the church.

What are you better after tonight
Than Ned the beggar or Seaghan the fool?

(from the Irish of Douglas Hyde)

Lady Gregory

His Answer when some Stranger
asked who he was

I am Raftery the poet, full of hope and love; my eyes without light, my gentleness without misery. Going west on my journey with the light of my heart; weak and tired to the end of my road.

I am now, and my back to a wall, playing music to empty pockets.

(from the Irish of Anthony Raftery 1784-1835)

Lady Gregory

The Old Woman of the Roads

Oh, to have a little house!
To own the hearth and stool and all!
The heaped-up sods upon the fire,
The pile of turf against the wall!

To have a clock with weights and chains
And pendulum swinging up and down,
A dresser filled with shining delph,
Speckled and white and blue and brown!

I could be busy all the day
Clearing and sweeping the hearth and floor,
And fixing on their shelf again
My white and blue and speckled store!

I could be quiet there at night
Beside the fire and by myself,
Sure of a bed and loath to leave
The ticking clock and the shining delph!

Och! but I'm weary of mist and dark,
And roads where there's never a house nor bush,
And tired I am of bog and road,
And the crying wind and the lonesome hush!

And I am praying to God on high,
And I am praying him night and day,
For a little house, a house of my own –
Out of the wind's and the rain's way.

Padraic Colum

A Piper

A Piper in the streets to-day
Set up, and tuned, and started to play,
And away, away, away on the tide
Of his music we started; on every side
Doors and windows were opened wide,
And men left down their work and came,
And women with petticoats coloured like flame
And little bare feet that were blue with cold,
Went dancing back to the age of gold,
And all the world went gay, went gay,
For half an hour in the street to-day.

Seumas O'Sullivan

The Sheep

Slowly they pass
In the grey of the evening
Over the wet road,
A flock of sheep.
Slowly they wend
In the grey of the gloaming
Over the wet road
That winds through the town.
Slowly they pass,
And gleaming whitely
Vanish away
In the grey of the evening.

Seumas O'Sullivan

The Find

I took a reed and blew a tune,
And sweet it was and very clear
To be about a little thing
That only few hold dear.

Three times the cuckoo named himself,
But nothing heard him on the hill,
Where I was piping like an elf
The air was very still.

'Twas all about a little thing
I made a mystery of sound,
I found it in a fairy ring
Upon a fairy mound. Knocacleva
Touching skies of gold and blue,
Easy hills of green and brown,
Lead the fairest water to
Hidden farm and valley town,
And the dew on fern and rock
Lingers until twelve o'clock.

When the beetles' wing is heard
Out upon the golden west,
And the golden-fluted bird
Stirs with beauty every breast,
The crow is home on the wooded hill,
Home in the marsh the whippoorwill.

Francis Ledwidge

Lullaby

Shall I take the rainbow out of the sky
And the moon from the well in the lane,
And break them in pieces to coax your eye
To slumber a wee while again?
Rock goes the cradle, and rock, and rock.
The mouse has stopped nibbling under the clock
And the crows have gone home to Slane.

The little lambs came from the hills of brown,
With pillows of wool for your fair little head.
And the birds from the bushes flew in with down
To make you snug in your cradle bed.
Rock goes the cradle, and rock, and rock.
The mouse has stopped nibbling under the clock.
And the birds and the lambs have fled.

There is wind from the bog. It will blow all night.
Upsetting the willows and scattering rain.
The poor little lambs will be crying with fright
For the kind little birds in the hedge of the lane.
Rock goes the cradle, and rock, and rock.
Sleep, little one, sleep, and the wet wind mock.
Till the crows come back from Slane.

Francis Ledwidge

To My Little Nephew Seumas
The Child of Dreams

I will bring you all the colours
Of the snail's house when I come,
And shells that you may listen
To a distant ocean's hum.
And from the rainbow's bottom
I will bring you coloured lights
To scare away the banshees
That cry in the nights.

And I will sing you strange songs
Of places far away,
Where little moaning waters
Have wandered wild astray.
'Till you shall see the bell flowers
Shaking in the breeze,
Thinking they are ringing them
The short way to the seas.

When I come back from wand'ring
It's the strange man I'll be,
And first you'll be a bit afraid
To climb upon my knee.
But when you see the rare gifts
I've gathered you, it seems
You'll lean your head upon me
And travel in your dreams.

Francis Ledwidge

My Mother

God made my mother on an April day,
From sorrow and the mist along the sea,
Lost birds' and wanderers' songs and ocean spray,
And the moon loved her wandering jealousy.

Beside the ocean's din she combed her hair,
Singing the nocturne of the passing ships,
Before her earthly lover found her there
And kissed away the music from her lips.

She came unto the hills and saw the change
That brings the swallow and the geese in turns.
But there was not a grief she deemed strange,
For there is that in her which always mourns.

Kind heart she has for all on hill or wave
Whose hopes grew wings like ants to fly away.
I bless the God who such a mother gave
This poor bird-hearted singer of a day.

Francis Ledwidge

Four Birds

Kestrel

In a sky ballroom
The kestrel
A stately dancer.
He is a true artist –
His art is not
divorced
From life
And death.

Owl

Night-winged
As a ghost
Or a gangster,
Mystical as a black priest
Reading the Devil's Mass.

Lark

Morning star
Announcing the birth
Of a love-child.

Corn-crake

A cry in the
wilderness
Of meadow.

Patrick Kavanagh

from *A Christmas Childhood*

I

One side of the potato-pits was white with frost –
How wonderful that was, how wonderful!
And when we put our ears to the paling-post
The music that came out was magical.

The light between the ricks of hay and straw
Was a hole in Heaven's gable. An apple tree
With its December-glinting fruit we saw –
O you, Eve, were the world that tempted me

To eat the knowledge that grew in clay
And death the germ within it! Now and then
I can remember something of the gay
Garden that was childhood's. Again

The tracks of cattle to a drinking-place,
A green stone lying sideways in a ditch
Or any common sight the transfigured face
Of a beauty that the world did not touch.

II

My father played the melodeon
Outside at our gate;
There were stars in the morning east
And they danced to his music.

Across the wild bogs his melodeon called
To Lennons and Callans.
As I pulled on my trousers in a hurry
I knew some strange thing had happened.

Outside in the cow-house my mother
Made the music of milking;
The light of her stable-lamp was a star
And the frost of Bethlehem made it twinkle.

A water-hen screeched in the bog,
Mass-going feet
Crunched the wafer-ice on the pot-holes,
Somebody wistfully twisted the bellows wheel.

My child poet picked out the letters
On the grey stone,
In silver the wonder of a Christmas townland,
The winking glitter of a frosty dawn.

Cassiopeia was over
Cassidy's hanging hill,
I looked and three whin bushes rode across
The horizon – the Three Wise Kings.

An old man passing said:
"Can't he make it talk" –
The melodeon. I hid in the doorway
And tightened the belt of my box-pleated coat.

I nicked six nicks on the door-post
With my penknife's big blade –
There was a little one for cutting tobacco.
And I was six Christmases of age.

My father played the melodeon,
My mother milked the cows,
And I had a prayer like a white rose pinned
On the Virgin Mary's blouse.

Patrick Kavanagh

What is Truth?

What is truth? says Pilate,
Waits for no answer;
Double your stakes, says the clock
To the ageing dancer;
Double the guard, says Authority,
Treble the bars;
Holes in the sky, says the child
Scanning the stars.

Louis MacNeice

Elephant Trunk

Descending out of the grey
Clouds elephant trunk
Twitches away
Hat;
THAT
Was not what I expected,
A
Misdirected
Joke it seemed to me;
"What about a levitation?" I had said,
Preening head for halo,
All alert, combed, sanctified,
I thank Thee, Lord, I am not like other men
WHEN
Descending out of the grey
Clouds elephant trunk . . .

(and so on
    ad nauseam)

Louis MacNeice

The Pet Shop

Cold blood or warm, crawling or fluttering
Bric-a-brac, all here to be bought,
Noisy or silent, python or myna,
Fish with long silk trains like dowagers,
Monkeys lost to thought.

In a small tank tiny enamelled
Green terrapin jostle, in a cage a crowd
Of small birds elbow each other and bicker
While beyond the ferrets eardrum, eyeball,
Find that macaw too loud.

Here behind glass lies a miniature desert,
The sand littered with rumpled gauze
Discarded by snakes like used bandages;
In the next door desert fossilized lizards
Stand in a pose, a pause.

But most of the customers want something comfy –
Rabbit, hamster, potto, puss –
Something to hold on the lap and cuddle
Making believe it will return affection
Like some neutered succubus.

Purr then or chirp, you are here for our pleasure,
Here at the mercy of our whim and purse;
Once there was the wild, now tanks and cages,
But we can offer you a home, a haven,
That might prove even worse.

Louis MacNeice

The Pet Shop

I never had the luck to keep a pet:
canary, rabbit, kitten, all were tried.
When she went mad, my father drowned the cat;
the rabbit fretted, the canaries died.

So, though my legs grew longer than my years,
I had no pup to race me round the hills.
The very sticklebacks brought home in jars,
within the week, were furred with fishy ills.

But when, on Saturdays, we went to town,
my chums and I, one window drew our gaze:
glass-tanks of snakes and lizards green and brown;
white mice and piebald mice on sawdust trays;
dumb tortoises; a haughty cockatoo;
bright, feathered bantams picking in the grit;
quick ferrets sniffing straw for something new,
and pigeons jerking on pink, clockwork feet.

Among the crowd that idled round the door,
you'd sometimes see a fellow slip his hand
into a hidden pocket to withdraw
a cowering lark or linnet contraband.

John Hewitt

The Owl

With quiet step and careful breath
we rubbered over grass and stone,
seeking that soft light-feathered bird
among the trees where it had flown.
The twisting road ran down beside
a straggling wood of ash and beech;
between us and the shadowed trees
a wire fence topped the whin-spiked ditch.
We stood and gazed: the only stir
of dry leaves in the topmost boughs;
the only noise now, far away,
the cawing of the roosting crows.
And as we watched in waning light,
our clenched attention pinned upon
that empty corner of the wood,
it seemed the quiet bird had gone.

Then when the light had ebbed to dusk
you moved a hand and signalled me:
I saw the little pointed ears
beside a tall and narrow tree.
A further signal, and I moved
in wide half-circle to surprise
that little feathered sheaf of life
that watched you watch with steady eyes.
But when I came by easy stealth,
at last, within a yard or two
the brown bird spread enormous wings
and rose and quietly withdrew.

And we were left to carry home
a sense no mortal will devised,
that, for one instant out of time,
we had been seen and recognised.

John Hewitt

Betrayal

I had a nurse when I was very small –
God only knows how we afforded her,
teachers' salaries being what they were.
Yet we lacked nothing much that I recall.

I loved her well. She always wore a hat,
and prammed me out along the afternoon,
from vast adventures coming home too soon.
My careless chatter put an end to that.

I learnt to talk apace. One fated day
my father asked me if the Park was fun.
The simple truth was that our steady run
was to a crony's house a mile away,
where I was loosed from harness and let out
to tumble with my cronies on the floor,
while one of our tall seniors went next door
and brought back six black bottles they called stout
and sweeties for the children. So I told
that we had been where stout and ladies were.
My father called the nurse in, being fair,
and, though he talked a long time, did not scold.

She combed my curls next day and went away,
and I was brokenhearted for a week.
That you should always think before you speak
was something which I learnt a later day.

John Hewitt

The Green Shoot

In my harsh city, when a Catholic priest,
known by his collar, padded down our street,
I'd trot beside him, pull my schoolcap off
and fling it on the ground and stamp on it.

I'd catch my enemy, that errand-boy,
grip his torn jersey and admonish him
first to admit his faith, and when he did,
repeatedly to curse the Pope of Rome;

schooled in such duties by my bolder friends;
yet not so many hurried years before,
when I slipped in from play one Christmas Eve
my mother bathed me at the kitchen fire,

and wrapped me in a blanket for the climb
up the long stairs; and suddenly we heard
the carol-singers somewhere in the dark,
their voices sharper, for the frost was hard.

My mother carried me through the dim hall
into the parlour, where the only light
upon the patterned wall and furniture
came from the iron lamp across the street;

and there looped round the lamp the singers stood,
but not on snow in grocers' calendars,
singing a song I liked until I saw
my mother's lashes were all bright with tears.

Out of this mulch of ready sentiment,
gritty with threads of flinty violence,
I am the green shoot asking for the flower,
soft as the feathers of the snow's cold swans.

John Hewitt

Wasps' Nest

This intricate construction,
delicate as tissue
woven of a myriad cells
hides in the larch trees' shelter.

It is a miniscule city
quivering in every fold
with knowledge of itself
and its own purpose.

If I approach,
a daggered sentinel
zips through the leaf-green air
to strike the foe
who menaces the waspish citadel.

Why did I not continue peaceably
about my private business?

Meta Mayne Reid

The Corncrake

Few see this creaking bird,
the crake, deep in meadow grass.
Even the kestrel cannot find
his speckled form among the swaying seeds.
The sun does not confound him,
and winds slide on like silver rain
over a swan's plumage.
He lives in an arcane habitat,
moving in secret ways,
stilt-legged in the clover mazes
of his emerald labyrinth,
rarely challenging the world
in an eccentric syncopation
of his harsh repeated cry.
He is the Holy Ghost of birds,
who, from obscurity,
cries havoc – or is it revelation?
for none but corncrake could translate
those enigmatic croaks from the field's heart

Meta Mayne Reid

The Whin Bush

Silk of the Kine?
Sorrowful Cathleen?
Little Old Woman away in the West?
You are not these, my country.
You are a whin bush,
indestructible,
bearing all weathers,
advancing insidiously
to claim the whole field
with a flare of orange,
a thrust of green
which stabs the thieving hand.
But – how sharp that scent,
how fierce the life which bursts
out of the gnarled root,
O whin bush wild in the green field.

Meta Mayne Reid

Three Year Old: Belfast 1972

She scarcely speaks,
wakes in the night screaming.

Yet she was fortunate
when the street exploded into flame.
She only took one bruise
though Mother was thrown to the wall,
the basket whirled into nothingness,
and the pram was crushed.

Now she expects
the whole world to explode again:

She hides her eyes and stares
into her bomb-blasted imagination.

Meta Mayne Reid

If I Knew

If I knew the box where the smiles are kept,
No matter how large the key,
Or strong the bolt I would try so hard
'Twould open I know for me,
Then over the land and sea broadcast
I'd scatter the smiles to play,
That the children's faces might hold them fast
For many and many a day.

If I knew the box that was large enough
To hold all the frowns I meet,
I would like to gather them every one
From the nursery, school or street,
Then, folding and holding, I'd pack them in
And turning the monster key,
I'd hire a giant to drop the box
To the depths of the deep, deep sea.

Anonymous

Section III

The Poets of Today

Biffety Boffety Boo!

Biffety Boffety Boo!
I'm gonna tickle you.
Outa the bed
You sleepyhead.
Biffety Boffety Boo!

Gabriel Fitzmaurice

My Hurley

Left! Right! Left! Right!
Marching down the hall,
My hurley as a rifle.
About turn at the wall!
I'm a soldier, Mammy.
(A hurley's best by far –
Today it can be a gun,
Tomorrow a guitar).

Gabriel Fitzmaurice

Water Babies

I'm a son
And you're a daughter
And we love
To mess with water
Shoes all squelchy
Hear them wheeze
Socks all sizzly
When we squeeze

Gabriel Fitzmaurice

Snots

Snots are gooey
Snots are sweet
Snots are chewy
Things to eat

Gabriel Fitzmaurice

How High?

How high can I piddle?
Higher than the door?
But the piddle hit it halfways up
And dribbled on the floor.

I got a ball of tissue
And rubbed the door till dry
And soaked it off the lino.
Wow! I can piddle high!

Gabriel Fitzmaurice

Dinosaur

I brought my dinosaur to school –
It was a Brontosaurus;
I played with it with my friend Jim,
But then the teacher saw us.

"Put that thing in", the teacher said,
"Or I'll put it in my drawer":
He only saw a plastic toy,
But I could hear it roar.

Gabriel Fitzmaurice

Cén Fáth?

Cén fáth cén fáth cén fáth cén fáth
A suíonn na fáinleoga gach aon lá
Thuas ar na sreanga in aon líne amháin
Cén fáth cén fáth cén fáth cén fáth?
Ag fanacht ar shreangscéal o na tíortha teo?
É! Nach bhfuil an t-ádh leo!

Why?

Why, why, why, why
Do the swallows sit high up on the wire
Each day in single line?
Why, why, why, why?
Waiting for a call from a warmer land?
O! Aren't they a happy band!

Gabriel Rosenstock
Trans Seán Hutton and Shaun Traynor

Galrollóir

Tá an galrollóir ag teacht,
Tá an galrollóir ag teacht,
As an tslí
A sheilidí
Tá an galrollóir ag teacht!

Tá an galrollóir ag teacht,
Tá an galrollóir ag teacht,
Teithigí
A phéistíní
Tá an galrollóir ag teacht!

Tá an galrollóir ag teacht,
Tá an galrollóir ag teacht,
Imigí
A fheithidí
Tá an galrollóir ag teacht!

Tá an galrollóir ag teacht,
Tá an galrollóir ag teacht,
Rithigí
A luchógaí
Tá an galrollóir ag teacht!

The Steamroller

The steamroller is coming,
The steamroller is coming,
Out of the way
You snails
The steamroller is coming!

The steamroller is coming,
The steamroller is coming,
Crawl fast
You worms
The steamroller is coming!

The steamroller is coming,
The steamroller is coming,
Clear off
You insects
The steamroller is coming!

The steamroller is coming,
The steamroller is coming,
Run away
You mice
The steamroller is coming!

Gabriel Rosenstock
Trans Seán Hutton and Shaun Traynor

An Smugairle Róin

Cén fáth a bhfuil tusa ag déanamh bróin?
A smugairle róin?
Cén fáth a bhfuil tusa ag déanamh bróin?

Cé a dúirt go bhfuil mise ag déanamh bróin?
Arsa an smugairle róin?
Cé a dúirt go bhfuil mise ag déanamh bróin?

Cad atá ar siúl agat, a smugairle róin?
Ag ithe do lóin?
Cad atá ar siúl agat, a smugairle róin?

Tá mé i mo shuí ar mo thóin,
Arsa an smugairle róin,
Ag ithe mo lóin is ag déanamh bróin
Agus beidh mé anseo go dtí – fan go bhfeicfidh mé
– ceathrú tar éis a ceathair, ar a laghad, san iarnóin.

The Jelly Fish

Why are you unhappy,
Little jelly fish?
Why are you
unhappy?

Who told you I'm unhappy?
Said the little jelly fish.
Who told you I'm unhappy?

What are you doing, little jelly fish?
Eating your lunch?
What are you doing, little jelly fish?

I'm sitting on my bum,
Said the little jelly fish,
Eating my lunch into my tum and being unhappy
And I shall be here – let me see – until kingdom come
Or at least 'til a quarter past four.

Gabriel Rosenstock
Trans Seán Hutton and Shaun Traynor

Dog in Space

The barking in space
has died out now,
though dogbones rattle.
And the marks of teeth
on the sputnik's hull
are proof of a battle
impossible to win.

And asteroid-dents
were no help at all.
Did the dog see,
through the window,
earth's blue ball?
Did the dog know
that no other dog
had made that circle
around the earth –
her historic spin
that turned eternal?

Matthew Sweeney

Flies Carry Flu

Flies carry flu,
especially the small ones,
the hardly-seen-at-all ones
that sit on your hair
and wait there.

They wait till you
laugh or yawn
or make a vowel sound.
They aim above your chin
and rush right in.

They die, of course.
Spittle kills them
but the germ survives them,
the flu germ
that does you harm.

That keeps getting better
at making you iller,
that could be a killer.
So in case you die
get that fly.

A girl I know
thinks a spider
permanently inside her
mouth might do it.
She wouldn't need to glue it

to the roof, she says,
and she wouldn't mind the thought
of a web in her throat.
That's not much to do
to avoid flu.

I don't agree.
I'm sure you know
better ways to go
about it, easier ways
to clobber flies

and keep out flu.
So why don't you write
a letter tonight
telling me how.

You can start right now.

Matthew Sweeney

Fishbones Dreaming

Fishbones lay in the smelly bin.
He was a head, a backbone and a tail.
Soon the cats would be in for him.

He didn't like to be this way.
He shut his eyes and dreamed back.

Back to when he was fat, and hot on a plate.
Beside green beans, with lemon juice
squeezed on him. And a man with a knife
and fork raised, about to eat him.

He didn't like to be this way.
He shut his eyes and dreamed back.

Back to when he was frozen in the freezer.
With lamb cutlets and minced beef and prawns.
Three months he was in there.

He didn't like to be this way.
He shut his eyes and dreamed back.

Back to when he was squirming in a net,
with thousands of other fish, on the deck
of a boat. And the rain falling
wasn't wet enough to breathe in.

He didn't like to be this way.
He shut his eyes and dreamed back.

Back to when he was darting through the sea,
past crabs and jellyfish, and others
like himself. Or surfacing to jump for flies
and feel the sun on his face.

He liked to be this way.
He dreamed hard to try and stay there.

Matthew Sweeney

Tortoise

I had
a pet
tortoise
oh
a pet
tortoise
like
nobody else's
(nobody
else
I
knew
had
a pet
tortoise).
His head
was hard
as bark
his neck
(underneath)
soft as
a trick
fountain-pen
snake's
his eyes
bird-bright.
I lacquered
his shell
to keep
it fresh.
He liked
fresh lettuce
ate it
voraciously
gallivanting round

the garden
more like
a hare than
a tortoise.
By night
I kept
him
in
a shed.
If I
forgot
maggots
crawled
next morning
inside
his shell
(I picked
them out
with a
match-stick).
In winter
he hiber
nated
in a
box
in
our
coal-shed
beside a
black heap
of top
quality
English
coal.
That
was his
undoing.

One morning
in February
I found
him
quite
dead
under
two chunks
of it.
A pre-fab
tortoise-backed
tortoise-slack
tomb.
I buried him
cried
lied
to myself
No more pets.
Next year
I bought
a goldfish
the next
a budgie
the next
a hamster
– all three
are since
dead.

Pets
(any more
than people)
are not
for keeps.

Beekeepers
yes

gamekeepers
park-keepers even
are aptly
named
bird-fanciers
greyhound-breeders
horse-owners
cat-lovers
falconers eve
– but who
ever heard
of a
tortoise
keeper?

Basil Payne

Dead Cat

Three boys
swinging
a dead cat
over a wall
do
you
find
that
funny?
I
don't
either
but
they didn't
look evil
to me
at all . . .

All
the same
they laughed
themselves silly
each time
the cat
didn't make it
over the wall
and cheered
when it did
at long last:
Heave-ho;
Heave-ho;
Hooray

One
Two

Three
And Away.
Maybe
(at that)
they weren't
guilty
maybe
the cat
simply died
of old age
distemper
pneumonia
heart-disease
maybe
the three
cat-swinging
cat-calling
boys
didn't
kill
it
at
all.

Anyway
they
got rid
of it
off the street
like good
upright
duty-doing
citizens
–   no more
offence to
sore eyes
of passers-by

(or spies).
Maybe
they laughed
simply
because
they
were just
as frightened
of death
as you
or I
(or even
the cat
was
before it
was dead).

What really
startles
is that
nothing
is as
dead as
a
dead
cat.

Basil Payne

A Colossal Glossary

The **aardvark**'s a kind of ant-eater, an "earth-pig" in Dutch,
while **abracadabra** is a charm much

favoured by alchemists.
As for that wine-coloured gem, the **amethyst,**

a Greek would place it in his cup "so as not to be drunk",
a thought no foul-mouthed **Anglo-Saxon** ever thunk.

Azure is the blue of lapis lazuli.
The **bandicoot** is a rat from Australasia

that likes to **browse** or graze on the tender shoots of rice.
A **carbon-copy**'s a replica, though only once or twice.

Yellow or green, **chartreuse** is a liqueur
distilled, as always, by monks. The **coypu**'s prized for its fur;

not so the wild dog or **dingo.**
An **eland**'s an African antelope. In medical lingo

an **epiglottis** is a tongue, an **esophagus** a gizzard.
A **glitch** would be a snag or hazard.

The **ibex** is a mountain goat; **i.e.** is short for **id est,**
in Latin "that is". A pain in the side

was once a **jade,** a word which
we now use of the greenish stone deemed to mend the stitch.

A **jennet** might also be a jade, in the horse-sense.
Soldiers in khaki uniforms tense

when they hear the siren-song of a **klaxon,**
since it almost always represents a call to action.

A **lagoon** is a shallow lake, usually on the coast.
The nocturnal **lemur** is essentially a ghost.

A Lilo is a rubber raft, while a **limousine**
is a vehicle whose occupants thankfully can't be seen

since they're often types who say moi for "me"
and have a penchant for drinking sparkling **mongoose**-pee.

Whipped cream is the main ingredient of **mousse.**
The **narwhal** relies on its tusk when hunting Eskimos.

Nebuchadnezzar was the king of Babylon
for whom the writing on the wall was plain

as plain can be; a **nicety** may be either a subtle
or idle distinction: as such, it's its own rebuttal.

The **oryx,** like all gazelles, is thought by lions to wallow
in self-pity. An **osier** is a type of willow.

A **pickle** is anything preserved in vinegar or brine.
As one pine opined to another pitch-pine,

"He that toucheth pitch shall be defiled";
though **pitch** more commonly refers to asphalt.

The root of **prehensile** is "prehendere", to seize;
you may already have grasped that a **quagga** is a wild ass.

The **rouble** and **rupee** are Russian and Indian coins.
To be **scrupulous** is to have qualms of conscience,

from "scrupulus", a stone with a cutting edge;
the reed with a razor-sharp blade is **sedge**.

Tamburlaine also known as Tamerlane or Timur,
was a Mongol king whose deportment was anything but demure,

his stock-in-trade being rapine and reprisal.
The **tapir** lives as a hermit in the rain-forests of Brazil

where it meditates on **Theology**;
"In the beginning was the Word, and the Word was Algae".

A no less avid theologian was Thomas de **Torquemada**
whose cruel streak ran the gamut

from burning at the stake through hanging by a gaff
to the flaying of some fatted divinity calf

all in the name of Truth and Justice.
On the subject of the "thrice-great" Hermes **Trismegistus,**

or his Lord Lieutenant, Zoroaster,
my lips are sealed. I will say this; a **trundle** is a caster.

Often mistaken for a llama or alpaca, the newly-shorn **vicuña**
spits at the thought of the Norseman or **Viking**

who stole the shirt off his back. The chief
sense of **winnow** is to fan, to separate the wheat from the chaff,

the sheep from the goats, good from evil.
It's hard to categorize the **xylophagan**, this wood-boring weevil
makes of something nothing, **zilch**;
just as a worm may contain an armada, little much,

so the meanings of all the rest
of the words in this book are buried in one, a treasurechest.

Paul Muldoon

Digging

Between my finger and my thumb
The squat pen rests; snug as a gun.

Under my window, a clean rasping sound
When the spade sinks into gravelly ground:
My father, digging. I look down
Till his straining rump among the flowerbeds
Bends low, comes up twenty years away
Stooping in rhythm through potato drills
Where he was digging.

The coarse boot nestled on the lug, the shaft
Against the inside knee was levered firmly.
He rooted out tall tops, buried the bright edge deep
To scatter new potatoes that we picked
Loving their cool hardness in our hands.

By God, the old man could handle a spade.
Just like his old man.

My grandfather cut more turf in a day
Than any other man on Toner's bog.
Once I carried him milk in a bottle
Corked sloppily with paper. He straightened up
To drink it, then fell to right away

Nicking and slicing neatly, heaving sods
Over his shoulder, going down and down
For the good turf. Digging.

The cold smell of potato mould, the squelch and slap
Of soggy peat, the curt cuts of an edge
Through living roots awaken in my head.
But I've no spade to follow men like them.

Between my finger and my thumb
The squat pen rests.
I'll dig with it.

Seamus Heaney

Mid-Term Break

I sat all morning in the college sick bay
Counting bells knelling classes to a close.
At two o'clock our neighbours drove me home.

In the porch I met my father crying –
He had always taken funerals in his stride –
And Big Jim Evans saying it was a hard blow.

The baby cooed and laughed and rocked the pram
When I came in, and I was embarrassed
By old men standing up to shake my hand
And tell me they were 'sorry for my trouble',
Whispers informed strangers I was the eldest,
Away at school, as my mother held my hand

In hers and coughed out angry tearless sighs.
At ten o'clock the ambulance arrived
With the corpse, stanched and bandaged by the
nurses.

Next morning I went up into the room. Snowdrops
And candles soothed the bedside; I saw him
For the first time in six weeks. Paler now,

Wearing a poppy bruise on his left temple,
He lay in the four foot box as in his cot.
No gaudy scars, the bumper knocked him clear.

A four foot box, a foot for every year.

Seamus Heaney

from *Markings*

We marked the pitch: four jackets for four square goalposts,
That was all. The corners and the squares
Were there like longitude and latitude
Under the bumpy thistly ground, to be
Agreed or disagreed about
When the time came. And then we picked the teams
And crossed the line our called names drew between us.

Youngsters shouting their heads off in a field
As the light died and they kept on playing
Because by then they were playing in their heads
And the actual kicked ball came to them
Like a dream heaviness, and their own hard
Breathing in the dark and skids on grass
Sounded like effort in another world . . .
It was quick and constant, a game that never need
Be played out. Some limit had been passed,
There was fleetness, furtherance, untiredness
In time that was extra, unforeseen and free . . .

Seamus Heaney

Lissadel

Long ago before the world began
there was Ireland
and we were children
walking there,
hand in hand.

We came to Lissadel
and coming up to noon
we met a man called Yeats who asked
if we believed in fairies;

We answered that we did
but only now and then
and when we were together.

"Once"
he said,
holding out his hand,
"Once I saw a fairy
no bigger than a fingerful of light
And instead of hair
had flowers growing out of its head
And if you'd care to wait
I'll go and find him
and fetch him in my cap?"

"Oh but we cannot wait,"
I said, "We must still
come through the night."
"Ugh!" says Yeats,
"I never fear the dark,
for what is the dark
but the tail end of the day
dyed black?" "Will you stop
and eat bread and drink white milk?"

"Oh but we cannot eat before the sun has set," I said.

"Well then," says he,
"I have nothing left to add."

Bowing, he left
and turned into the road that leads to the World's End
and we came out of it laughing;

Concerned with what we had seen and heard,
how we had come to spend a day at Lissadel
and how that no-one – not even he –

knew who we were.

Madge Herron

Poem Without Title

I am above the eagle bearing west.
Is he blue?
He is the blue of rooftops.
Have you seen God?
I have.
What is God like?
He is large and wears a shade across his face at noon.
Where are you going?
I'm going to the sun.
Is the eagle's nest there?
It is.
The eagle's nest is there, it is hidden in the sun.

Madge Herron

Legends

Tryers of firesides
twilights. There are no tears in these.

Instead, they begin the world again,
making the mountain ridges blue
and the rivers clear and the hero fearless

and the outcome always undecided
so the next teller can say begin and
again and astonish children.

Our children are our legends.
You are mine. You have my name.
My hair was once like yours.

And the world
is less bitter to me
because you will re-tell the story.

Eavan Boland

Poem from a Three-Year-Old

And will the flowers die?

And will the people die?

And every day do you grow old, do I
grow old, no I'm not old, do
flowers grow old?

Old things – do you throw them out?

Do you throw old people out?

And how you know a flower that's old?

The petals fall, the petals fall from flowers,
and do the petals fall from people too,
every day more petals fall until the
floor where I would like to play I
want to play is covered with old
flowers and people all the same
together lying there with petals fallen
on the dirty floor I want to play
the floor you come and sweep
with the huge broom.

The dirt you sweep, what happens that,
what happens all the dirt you sweep
from flowers and people, what
happens all the dirt? Is all the
dirt what's left of flowers and
people, all the dirt there in a
heap under the huge broom that
sweeps everything away? Why you work so hard, why brush
and sweep to make a heap of dirt?

And who will bring new flowers?

And who will bring new people? Who will
bring new flowers to put in water
where no petals fall on to the
floor where I would like to
play? Who will bring new flowers
that will not hang their heads
like tired old people wanting sleep?
Who will bring new flowers that
do not split and shrivel every
day? And if we have new flowers
will we have new people too to
keep the flowers alive and give
them water?

And will the new young flowers die?

And will the new young people die?

And why?

Brendan Kennelly

*This poem is based on the bewildered outbursts and splutterings of
a three-year-old child during a period of about two weeks when,
for the first time, she became conscious of the fact of death. That
consciousness soon passed, to be replaced by the habitual
unawareness common to us all. During those two weeks, however, I
wrote down some of the excited, rather frightened phrases uttered
by the child. These phrases form the basis of this poem which
subsequently I re-wrote many times.*
Brendan Kennelly

The Big 'Un

The most promising, challenging thing in the world –
A mind of your own.

Ashington! Ashington!
Charlton! Charlton!

His mother called him the big 'un
Bobby his brother she called the little 'un
and when she asked the big 'un
to look after the little 'un
the big 'un liked to go off on his own

          wander away on his own

           wander away from home

      to find himself
      in his own time
      in his own way,

      the big 'un
      with a mind of his own!

When he was fifteen
he went down in the coal-pit

the cold, lonely pit
took one long look at it

and left it for good
yes, left it for good
and played football instead
(Thank God!   Thank God!)

'cos he had a mind of his own
in that tough, thoughtful head.

I don't believe in luck, he said,
There's only work, he said,
work
in summer and winter light.

And there's only one thing to do –
do the job right!

So it's Ireland one
Italy none.
He does the job right!

Orlando and the heat,
the fierce killing heat
and the sweat of defeat –

Mexico two
Ireland one.

There's a job to be done!

Fined ten grand, banned
from the sideline after Orlando,
Jack directs the play from the stand
in New York,
a phone in his hand.

He knows what he wants to do –
enjoy a beer
and a different point of view!

Ireland nil.
Norway nil

and we're through
to Round Two!

Back to Orlando and the heat
and the Dutch scoring two to our nil,

bitter pill,
this is the moment when

it's time for home
and the party in the Park
for Jack and his men.

You defined this island for a while, Jack.

Thank you

for all the happy madness,
the laughing squandering,
stranger talking to stranger
like brother to sister
sister to brother

Thank you for all the midnight fun,
how you could pour
abandon through the summer of '94,
making spoilsport time
weave and sprint and run

and set the people of this island

singing and dancing in the sun.

The people know what you want to do
after all their well-wishing
to you:

Wander away on your own,
big 'un.

It's time to go fishin'.

Brendan Kennelly

Cantona

One touch, then turn, then open the defence,
Then, gliding down your private corridor,
Arriving as the backs go screaming out,
You slide into slow motion as you score
Again, in the heroic present tense.
As Trevor says, that's what it's all about.

Like boxing and the blues, it's poor man's art.
It's where the millions possess a gift
As vital as it looks vicarious:
While Fergie chews and struts like Bonaparte
We see the pride of London getting stiffed,
And victory falls on the Republic, us.

But Eric, what about that Monsieur Hyde,
Your second half, who grows Les Fleurs du Mal
Who shows his studs, his fangs and his disdain,
Who gets sent off, then nearly sent inside
For thumping jobsworths at the Mondiale?
Leave thuggery to thugs and use your brain:
Now choose the spot before the ball arrives,
Now chest it, tee it, volley from the D.
Now Wimbledon, like extras, simply look,
And even Hansen feels he must agree:
This "luxury" is why the game survives,
This poetry that steps outside the book.

Sean O'Brien

The Trout

Flat on the bank I parted
Rushes to ease my hands
In the water without a ripple
And tilt them slowly downstream
To where he lay, tendril light
In his fluid sensual dream.

Bodiless lord of creation
I hung briefly above him
Savouring my own absence
Senses expanding in the slow
Motion, the photographic calm
That grows before action.

As the curve of my hands
Swung under his body
He surged, with visible pleasure.
was so preternaturally close
I could count every stipple
But still cast no shadow, until

The two palms crossed in a cage
Under the lightly pulsing gills.
Then (entering my own enlarged
Shape, which rode on the water)
I gripped. To this day I can
Taste his terror on my hands.

John Montague

A Grafted Tongue

(Dumb,
bloodied, the severed
head now chokes to
speak another tongue –

As in
a long suppressed dream,
some stuttering garb-
led ordeal of my own)

An Irish
child weeps at school
repeating its English.
After each mistake

The master
gouges another mark
on the tally stick
hung about its neck

Like a bell
on a cow, a hobble
on a straying goat.
To slur and stumble

In shame
the altered syllables
of your own name:
to stray sadly home

And find
the turf-cured width
of your parents' hearth

growing slowly alien: In cabin
and field, they still
speak the old tongue.
You may greet no one.

To grow
a second tongue, as
harsh a humiliation
as twice to be born.

Decades later
that child's grandchild's
speech stumbles over lost
syllables of an old order.

John Montague

Time Out

The donkey sat down on the roadside
Suddenly, as though tired of carrying
His cross. There was a varnish
Of sweat on his coat, and a fly
On his left ear. The tinker
Beating him finally gave in,
Sat on the grass himself, prying
His coat for his pipe. The donkey
(not beautiful but more fragile
than any swan, with his small
front hooves folded under him)
Gathered enough courage to raise
That fearsome head, ripping a daisy,
As if to say – slowly, contentedly –
Yes, there is a virtue in movement,
But only going so far, so fast,
Sucking the sweet grass of stubbornness.

John Montague

Finn and the Salmon of Knowledge

Long ago, beneath the sea,
There grew a magic hazel-tree.
Its nuts, enchanted by a spell,
Had Knowledge hidden in the shell.
The tree stood very near a well,
And there a salmon used to dwell.

He didn't need to go to school,
For when the nuts fell in the pool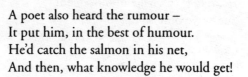
He ate them up, and said with glee:
"I really fancy nuts for tea –
And thanks to all those tasty dishes
I'm now the brainiest of fishes!"

A poet also heard the rumour –
It put him, in the best of humour.
He'd catch the salmon in his net,
And then, what knowledge he would get!

Finegas was the poet's name –
To everybody he'd proclaim:
"I am the best and brightest bard
From Aughnacloy to Oughterard!"

For seven years time seemed to crawl,
And still, the salmon didn't call.
The poet got a bit depressed
Until one day he had a guest:
"My name" he said, "is Finn Mac Cool,
And I would like to go to school
And learn to be a proper poet.
If there's a way, I'm sure you know it.

Finegas shook him by the hand:
"I am the finest in the land.
If poetry is your delight,
I'll teach you how to write it right!"
And so Finn stayed and studied hard
To learn the secrets of the Bard.

One day he looked into the river
And saw a sight that made him quiver:
A silver salmon, huge and proud,
Was talking to himself out loud!

Finn listened, then began to shout:
"That's what I'll write an ode about!
To find a real live talking salmon
Is like being given bread with jam on!
Perhaps I'll join him for a swim:
I'd really learn a lot from him!"

Finegas heard his cries of joy.
He said: "That Salmon's mine, my boy!
I've waited seven years to meet it –
And now at last I'm going to eat it!
This river bank will be the venue:
Don't write an ode, just write the menu!"

The cunning bard said: "Salmon dear,
From what you say, it's very clear
That you're the wisest fish around."
"If any wiser can be found,"
The salmon said, "Then I'm a clam!
A genius is what I am –
My brain's the most enormous size."
"Then," said the Bard, "you get the prize!"

The salmon said, "A prize, no less!
What can it be? Now let me guess.
A bowl of worms? A cup? A shield?
A holiday in Sellafield?"

The poet said, with hungry eyes:
"It is a Bumper Mystery Prize.
You wonder now, what can it be?
Then come up here, and you will see!"

The salmon knew the risk he took
In popping up to take a look . . .

This is an excerpt from a longer poem; "The Cool MacCool" by Gordon Snell.

Gordon Snell

The Reading Lesson

Fourteen years old, learning the alphabet,
He finds letters harder to catch than hares
Without a greyhound. Can't I give him a dog
To track them down, or put them in a cage?
He's caught in a trap, until I let him go,
Pinioned by "Don't you want to learn to read?"
"I'll be the same man whatever I do."

He looks at a page as a mule balks at a gap
From which a goat may hobble out and bleat.
His eyes jink from a sentence like flushed snipe
Escaping shot. A sharp word, and he'll mooch
Back to his piebald mare and bantam cock.
Our purpose is as tricky to retrieve
As mercury from a smashed thermometer.

"I'll not read any more." Should I give up?
His hands, long-fingered as a Celtic scribe's,
Will grow callous, gathering sticks or scrap;
Exploring pockets of the horny drunk
Loiterers at the fairs, giving them lice.
A neighbour chuckles. "You can never tame
The wild-duck: when his wings grow, he'll fly off."
If books resembled roads, he'd quickly read:
But they're small farms to him, fenced by the page.
Ploughed into lines, with letters drilled like oats:
A field of tasks he'll always be outside.
If words were bank-notes, he would filch a wad;
If they were pheasants, they'd be in his pot
For breakfast or if wrens he'd make them king.

Richard Murphy

An tUlchabhán

Ní cheapfá gurbh éan creiche é
'gus an eitilt spadánta sin faoi,
é go taibhsiúil sa chlapsholas
os cionn an mhóinín bháin.
Ansin, de thoirt, chrom sé ar an bhfiach.
Nuair a dhíríomar soilse an chairr air
chas sé a cheann go sotalach,
ag díriú orainn, gan loiceadh,
na súile móra ar leathadh –
ag casadh ár ndánachta linn.
Is siúd arís e i mbun ghnó golb is crúibe
roimh éirí ar a chaoithiúlacht:
an tseilg i gerucaí an stiallaire.

The owl

You'd never guess it was a bird of prey,
flying languidly,
ghost-like in the dusk
above the grass verge.
Then, like a flash, he struck.
When we fixed the headlights on him
he turned his head, disdainfully
fixing those big, unflinching
wide-open eyes upon us –
contemptuous of our audacity.
Then he resumed his work with beak and claw
before rising, just when it suited him:
a destroyer clutching his prey.

Seán Hutton

In Memory of James Glackin: "Do not go gently into that good night"

You went on a
Christmas day
Your own Holy Day
You didn't forget
me.
I was in Dundalk
when the phone
rang with your
message. Thanks
for arranging with the
Holy Spirit that the boat
from Ireland would be in time
for me to hear
Mass before
your long holiday.
No doubt
you have had a reunion with the family;
how's granny?
Tell Uncle Paddy I've
got a great book
Greyhound for
Breakfast
I am sure he can get it from
God's library.
And my last request tell
Mother not
to forget to say
a novena for her
mad son Eddie.

Eddie Linden

The Aspidistra
(For Jane and Nellie)

In an alcove on the landing
stood a plant without a flower;
a polished aspidistra
in a purple Chinese jar.

On wet April evenings
or early in July, we'd jump
the first steep flight of stairs
and play there near the sky.

It was our favourite hideout
far from school and church and bars,
or the raspy Belfast voices
raised in anger down the stairs.

And if the priest or sergeant
paid their weekly social call,
two cousins and their sisters
fled the mosaic marbled hall.

One evening in October not
far from All Souls' Night,
granda told us stories which
made hair itch with fright.

One was of the landing where
a sickened man had died,
found hanging in the morning
by aunts who screeched and lied.

His eyes had popped their sockets,
his face was darkly pale, and when
they cut his dead weight down
they hammered in the nails.

But very shortly after
a strange event occurred,
the spreading aspidistra
dropped dying near the birds.

It lay like that for seasons
its flesh a sickly grey, but on
the following All Souls' Night
its leaves put on display.

It grew and grew much stronger
its sheen the deepest green,
and for sixty long years after
mocked the hanging beam.

When his story ended,
with faces scared and red,
we eyed one another and
quietly stole to bed.

No standing at the doorway
or talking to the jar,
or playing in a garden of
Chinese petalled flowers,

but straight to bed to shiver
in a darkness near complete,
but for a shaft of gaslight
from the landing near our feet.

Tom Morgan

Nothing is Safe

Nothing is safe anymore.
I wrote a poem last night
And when I woke up this morning
There was no sign of it.

I thought the mice had eaten it
(We're subject to mice in this house)
But then again
Why should they?
Poetry doesn't agree with mice.

Of course,
The present climate being
What it is
Anything may have happened –
sudden rain storm
During the night
The cold air
Thieving through the window
And the poem dies of pneumonia.

Next time I write a poem
I'll send it to my aunt
Who lives in a madhouse.
She's blind
But she likes the texture of
paper.
She holds it in her hand
Crinkles it up
And listens to the sound.

Perhaps
That's all that
matters
in the end –
The sound of paper
Screaming in the hand.

Patrick Galvin

Biographical Index: Section I

THE HERMIT'S SONG (Anonymous). This poem was written in the seventh century. It gives us a very clear vision of what Ireland was like then. The hermit was, in fact, a rather special person. His name was Marbhan and he was brother to King Guaire.

FRANK O'CONNOR (Translator) was born Cork in 1903. He wrote novels and short stories and was a director of the Abbey Theatre. He spent some years in England and in America where he lectured at Harvard. He died in 1966 in Dublin.

THE FOUR SEASONS (Anonymous). The text of these poems was found in an eighteenth century tale but they are thought to date from the eleventh century or even earlier.

COLUM CILLE'S FAREWELL TO IRELAND. This poem is attributed to the saint who lived in the sixth century. In its original Irish it contains one of the most famous lines in ancient literature: "My name, I don't conceal it: Back turned towards Ireland." It is the lament of one of the first emigrants, so upset about leaving Ireland that he re-names himself, "He who set his back toward Ireland."

I'VE NEWS FOR YOU (Anonymous). In this poem the poet gives us an insight into what Ireland was like at the time. The poem dates back to the ninth or tenth century (maybe even earlier).

THE SCHOLAR AND HIS CAT. This poem was written by an Irish monk in a monastery in Austria in the ninth century.

While working on a religious manuscript he nightly observed his cat who was his only companion. He became inspired to write this poem which he scribbled in the margin of the larger manuscript. So it has survived.

ICHAM OF IRLAUNDE An important milestone in the history of Irish Literature since it is thought to be the first poem written in English in Ireland.

Biographical Index: Section II

CECIL FRANCES ALEXANDER was born at Humphreys in County Wicklow in 1818 but spent most of her adult life in the North of Ireland. She married William Alexander in 1851, after her most famous hymns were already written. "Once in Royal David's City", "All Things Bright and Beautiful", and "There is a Green Hill Far Away" were included in *Hymns for Little Children* (1848) which she wrote for her Sunday School in Strabane. She died in 1895 in Derry, where her husband was bishop. He afterwards became Archbishop of Armagh.

WILLIAM ALLINGHAM was born in Ballyshannon, County Donegal, in 1824 and served as a customs official at posts all over the North of Ireland. He went to live in England and was a friend of Tennyson. He died in 1889 and was buried in Ballyshannon.

JOSEPH CAMPBELL was born in Belfast in 1879. He was part of the Ulster Literary Revival. His main interest was in poetry and in collecting songs. He died in Glencree in 1944.

AUSTIN CLARK was born in Dublin 1896 and lived for most of his boyhood in Mountjoy Street near the Black Church (St

Mary's Chapel of Ease) and was educated at University College, Dublin. He died in 1974.

PADRAIC COLUM was born Patrick McCormac Colm in Longford in 1881, the son of a workhouse master. A novelist, playwright and poet, he was an important figure in the Irish Literary Renaissance. His later life was spent in America where he became an authority on folklore. He died in Connecticut and was buried in Sutton, County Dublin in 1972.

OLIVER GOLDSMITH was born in 1728 in Pallasmore, County Longford, the son of a local curate. He was educated at Trinity College and studied medicine in Edinburgh and Leyden in Holland. He wrote *The Vicar of Wakefield* (1776), *The Deserted Village* (1770) and *She Stoops to Conquer* (1778), one each of the most famous novels, poems and plays in English. He died of a fever in London in 1774.

LADY AUGUSTA GREGORY was born in 1852 in County Galway and died in Coole Park in 1932. She was described by GB Shaw as "the greatest living Irishwoman".

JOHN HEWITT was born in Belfast in 1907 and educated at Queen's University. In 1930 he joined the staff of the Belfast Museum and later moved to Coventry to administer an Art Gallery. He died in Belfast in 1987.

JAMES JOYCE was born in Dublin in 1882 but lived most of his life abroad. He died in Switzerland in 1941.

PATRICK KAVANAGH was born in Inishkeen, County Monaghan in 1904 and lived there as farmer, cobbler and poet until his move to Dublin in 1939. When he died in 1967 he was regarded as one of Ireland's finest poets.

ADELAIDE O'KEEFFE was born in 1776. She was the daughter of John O'Keeffe, a writer of farces and comic operas. He came to London from Dublin in 1770 to seek his fortune. In 1797 he became blind and Adelaide, his only daughter, looked after him. During this time she wrote books of poems for children which were published during her lifetime. She died in 1885.

FRANCIS LEDWIDGE was born in Slane, County Meath, in 1891. He worked in the fields and on roadworks and was uneducated in the accepted sense of the word. His writing of poetry was greatly encouraged by Lord Dunsany, the local landlord. Tragically, Ledwidge joined the British army in the First World War and was killed in Flanders in 1917.

WINIFRED M LETTS was born in Dublin in 1882 and was educated at Alexandra College. She contributed several plays to the early Abbey repertoire and wrote many stories for children. She married WHF Vershoyle. She died in 1950.

MARY DAVENPORT O'NEILL was born in Loughrea, County Galway, in 1893. She was educated at the National College of Art and married the historical novelist, Joseph O'Neill. She wrote several verse plays and some poetry but was chiefly famous for her Dublin literary salon. She died in 1967.

PADRAIC PEARSE was born in Dublin in 1879. he is perhaps best known as a patriot for his part in the Easter Rising of 1916. He was also a poet and ran his own school, St Enda's, in Rathfarnham. He was executed in 1916.

META MAYNE REID was born in Yorkshire to Irish parents in 1905. She graduated from the University of Manchester. From 1930 onwards most of her life was spent in Belfast. During her varied career she worked as a journalist, with a brief period as a sports correspondent for the *Times of India*. She married in 1935 and had a lifelong interest in Ireland and Irish folklore. She is the author of 24 children's books and three adult novels. She died in 1990.

ELIZABETH SHANE was born Gertrude Elizabeth Heron Ilind, in Belfast in 1877. She published several volumes of verse about West Donegal. She had a much greater impact than many a more famous writer with her recitation "Wee Hughie" which was known to generations of Northern schoolchildren. She died in 1951.

ARTHUR O'SHAUGHNESSY was born in London of Irish parents in 1844. He worked as a transcriber in the British Museum and afterwards in the National History Department when it was transferred to South Kensington. He died in 1881.

JAMES STEPHENS was born in Dublin in 1881. Though he had no formal education, he rose in the literary world much encouraged by the Dublin poet, AE (George Russell). His most famous book is *A Crock of Gold*. He died in 1950.

SEAMUS O'SULLIVAN is the pen name of James Sullivan Starkey who was born in Dublin in 1879. He was for many years the editor of a literary journal, *The Dublin Magazine*. He died in 1958.

JONATHAN SWIFT was born in Dublin in 1667. He was the greatest satirist of his age and the author of *Gulliver's Travels*. He was also Dean of St Patrick's cathedral in Dublin. He died in 1745.

WB YEATS was born in Dublin in 1865. He is possibly Ireland's most famous poet. He won the Nobel Prize for literature in 1923. He founded the Abbey Theatre together with Lady Gregory and became a Senator of the Irish Free State. He died in France in 1939. He is buried in County Sligo.

EAVAN BOLAND was born in Dublin in 1944. She has lived in Ireland, London and New York. She has published many volumes of poetry and is a leading voice in contemporary Irish writing. She lives and works in Dublin.

GABRIEL FITZMAURICE was born in 1952 in Moyvane, County Kerry where he lives and teaches in the local national school. He is the author of more than twenty books, among them poetry for adults and children's verse in English and Irish. Among his books for children are *The Moving Stair* and *But Dad!*, both published by Poolbeg Press.

PATRICK GALVIN was born in Cork in 1927. He is a dramatist and a poet. He has held several positions as writer-in-residence in Britain and Ireland. He lives in Cork.

SEAMUS HEANEY was born on a farm in County Derry in 1939. He was educated at St Columb's College and Queen's University Belfast. He is Ireland's leading living poet. He has taught at Queen's University, Belfast, and now teaches at Yale and Oxford. In 1996 he won the Nobel Prize for poetry.

MADGE HERRON was born in Donegal in 1916 but has lived in England for most of her adult life. She comes from the oral tradition and very few of her poems have been written down, and none have been published in book form.

SEÁN HUTTON was born in 1940 in Dublin. He is a poet and a translator. London-based, he is Chairman of The British Association for Irish Studies. He is also Secretary of the Irish Texts Society.

BRENDAN KENNELLY was born in Kerry in 1936. He was educated at Trinity College, Dublin, where he now teaches and is a Senior Fellow. He is the author of many collections of poetry. He lives and works in Dublin.

EDDIE LINDEN was born in Coalisland in County Tyrone in 1935 but moved to Scotland when he was very young. Of humble parentage, he had many early hardships to overcome. He won a place at Ruskin College, Oxford, and now lives in London where he founded the now well established poetry magazine, *Aquarius*. In 1995 a play about him, *Who is Eddie Linden?* was performed in Edinburgh and London.

LOUIS MacNEICE was born in Belfast in 1907, the son of an Anglican rector. He was educated at Marlborough College in Wiltshire and at Oxford University. He had a distinguished career in the BBC and is one of Ulster's leading poets. He died in 1963.

JOHN MONTAGUE was born to a farming family in County Tyrone in 1929. He was educated at University College, Dublin, and at York University. He lives and works in Cork.

TOM MORGAN was born in Ligoniel, Northern Ireland. He taught for twenty years in a secondary school in Belfast where he was head of English.

PAUL MULDOON was born in 1951 in Northern Ireland. This glossary to his first book for children, The Last Thesaurus, published by Faber & Faber, is a poem in itself. He now lectures in America.

RICHARD MURPHY was born in Galway in 1927 and spent much of his early life in Ceylon. He has travelled the world but has now returned to Ireland. He lives and works in County Dublin.

SEAN O'BRIEN was born in 1952 in London. He is second generation Irish, lives in England and is a poetry critic for *The Sunday Times*.

BASIL PAYNE was born in Dublin in 1928. A critic and translator as well as a poet, he has lived in Germany and the United States.

GABRIEL ROSENSTOCK was born in 1949. He is the author/translator of over seventy books. Some of his children's titles include *Deanta Duitse* (CIC), *The Confessions of Henry Hooter the Third* (Brandon), *Fear na bPéistíní* (CIC), *An Phéist Mhór* (An Gúm). He currently works for An Gúm.

GORDON SNELL was born in Singapore and spent much of his childhood in Australia. He has written many poems, song lyrics and librettoes as well as books of poetry for children, from one of which the poem about "The Salmon of Knowledge" is taken. Gordon has been resident in Ireland for many years and now lives in County Dublin. He is married to the writer Maeve Binchy.

MATTHEW SWEENEY was born in Donegal in 1952. He is one of Ireland's leading younger poets. He lives in London and was writer-in-reidence at London's South Bank Arts Centre in 1994/5.

Acknowledgements

For kind permission to reprint copyright material, acknowledgement is made to the following:

The Society of Authors for poems by James Stephens. AP Watt for poems by WB Yeats. Maire Colum O'Sullivan for "The Old Woman of the Roads" by Padraic Colum. Mrs Katherine Kavanagh and Mr Peter Fallon as the agent for the literary estate of Patrick Kavanagh for poems by Patrick Kavanagh. The author and Gallery Press for poems by John Montague. David Highams Ltd for poems by Louis MacNeice. The author and Blackstaff Press for poems by John Hewitt. Poolbeg Press and the author for poems by Gabriel Fitzmaurice. The author for poems by Gabriel Rosenstock. Faber & Faber and the authors for poems by Seamus Heaney, Paul Muldoon and Matthew Sweeney. The representatives of the author for poems by Madge Herron. The author for "Legends" by Eavan Boland. The author for "The Big 'Un" by Brendan Kennelly and the author and Bloodaxe books for "Poem from a Three-Year-Old" by Brendan Kennelly. The author for "The Reading Lesson" by Richard Murphy. The author for "In Memory of James Glackin Quinn" by Eddie Linden. Dr Mark Read for poems by Meta Mayne Reid. Oxford University Press and the author for "Cantona" by Sean O'Brien.

While every attempt has been made to contact all copyright holders, Poolbeg Press and Shaun Traynor apologise for any errors or omissions in the above list. We would be happy to be notified of any corrections to be incorporated in the next edition.